fresh courage

to believe

Lenore C. Uddyback-Fortson

Thoughts

My vision for _fresh courage to believe_ grew out of my impatience, and the frustration I consistently felt (and sometimes still feel) transitioning from one stage of life to another. This collection of poems reflects the myriad of emotions that come from that frustration and often bubble to the surface, as well as the new mercies and unending grace God continues to show me in spite of me.

I commit this work to my Lord and Savior, Jesus Christ, without whom, nothing is possible. I dedicate this book to the men in my life—my husband, Wes and my son, Noah—who unconditionally love me through this life journey, lifting my spirits and making me laugh along the way. I present this book to you, the reader, and pray it is edifying, offering you words of encouragement, as well as fresh insight.

Table of Contents

Because of the LORD's great love, we are not consumed, for his compassions never fail. They are new every morning; great is your faithfulness. I say to myself, "The LORD is my portion; therefore, I will wait for him."

Lamentations 3:22-24 (NIV)

The stillness
that consumes the earliest part of the day;
with morning's silent hello
makes every hope seem possible;
leaves room for every dream to come true.

But these are written that you may believe that Jesus is the Messiah, the Son of God, and that by believing you may have life in his name.

John 20:31 (NIV)

believe

I have seen
visions manifest;
intense high-definition dreams,
channeling
a steady stream
of slight vibrations to my spirit,
amplified internal echoes,
progress in surround sound.
once wistful,
nearly left-by-the-wayside wishes
transformed
by indestructible intention.

I've felt the Hand of God
pick me up,
propel me forward
snatched from the jaws of doubt
before defeat could devour;
my steps, ordered,
redirected to fall
in a new line of succession,
reconstructing
a once-broken trajectory
smoothing the surface,
straightening a crooked path.

I've sensed my Savior's presence
wrapped in an ever-loving embrace
that shields my heart
in the midst of madness,
comforting me
during every dark, déjà vu moment.

I've witnessed
a fleeting glimpse
of promise materialize
in the formation of my purpose;
watched fears blow like smoke,
sending rings of false truth
into the atmosphere
when I surrendered
self-imposed obstacles,
laid down any barrier to trust
resisting every attempt
to steal, kill, destroy my future, and
silenced faith's inner critic,
awakening my fiercest warrior who
rises,
emboldened by
fresh courage to believe.

For we are God's handiwork, created in
Christ Jesus to do good works, which God prepared
in advance for us to do.

Ephesians 2:10 (NIV)

handiwork

God read my heart last night,
or should I say He readied my heart
while I cowered in my thoughts
feeling raggedy
tattered, troubled
trippin' over poor decision,
after poor decision,
after missed opportunity, after…
my steps halted
by defeat's deflection

yet while I retraced all those missteps,
He lovingly traced over
every nuance of my unspoken dreams
and gave new life
to the power of intention
positioning His plan
dead center
for my full view

in a sleep haze
I instantly recognized His hand on my life,
sensed the reflection of His handiwork
electrifying my desire

to move forward, closer to
His vision
ready to roll up my sleeves
and dig into the good work

Brothers and sisters, I do not consider myself yet to have taken hold of it. But one thing I do: Forgetting what is behind and straining toward to what is ahead, I press on toward the goal to win the prize for which God has called me heavenward in Christ Jesus.

Philippians 3:13-14 (NIV)

battle on

I know what it's like
to feel cemented to the status quo
with no clear escape plan
sidelined by life,
swallowed whole by circumstances;
riddled with the consequence of inaction,
trapped somewhere between
the unrelenting echo of regret
and the hope of a new day,
hiding just beyond
the other side of midnight.

I can relate when you say
you're strapped,
choking on the dust of
fleeting resources,
left weary by the taunt of the slightest challenge;
legs giving out under the weight of unmet
responsibility and unrealized dreams.

I remember finally pushing past
my latest self-fulfilling defeat,
only to slip, lose footing and find myself
accelerating backward
to emotional quicksand;

whipped on a continuous loop,
uncompromising vertigo.

I understand the layers of this heartache,
so I battle on
in full armor;
press, choosing to fight through
the urge to succumb to my feelings.

taking my cue from that still small voice,
I summon mustard-seed faith
to put off the past
and wrap myself in God's plan--a path of life
that points to an expected end,
sacred steps leading to my destiny.

I search until I find
the courage to believe His promises
shining through the intricacies that reflect
His fearfully and wonderfully made creation,
embracing my rightful place
within a royal priesthood.

I take refuge under His wings as
He covers me with His feathers
and shields me with His faithfulness;
draw strength as

I remain still, doubts quieted,
knowing He is God.

I cling to His peace,
as it transcends all understanding,
soothing unexpected travails
braced by a stance
that informs my journey
as I set out
to seize unmet terrain
with renewed energy
and revel in,
time redeemed.

We demolish arguments and every pretension that sets itself up against the knowledge of God, and we take captive every thought to make it obedient to Christ

2 Corinthians 10:5 (NIV)

full blast

If our thoughts were on full blast
laid bare for all to see
our slightest inclinations
exposed raw
in the absence of
pious pretense,
just plain glimpses of an image
devoid of a skewed sense of self,
what would they reveal?

would they offer
a more honest view
of our overall outlook,
rock the foundation
of every shaky self-proclamation,
unravel the protective covering
equipped with all the proper platitudes,
tear at the seams of the pasted smile
that appears on cue
resolved to avoid sharing true feelings
or admit everything isn't always fine?

would they provide perspective
to curate the elements of character?

unleash an incognito ego
while removing all traces
of false humility consistently used
to push back against
the perpetual rising tide of insecurity?
would we still rush
to shun the suggested sins of others,
knowing ours were unmasked
no longer denied?
instead cowering
in fear of judgement,
marked by shame?

if we basked in unfiltered rays of truth,
intentionally radiating an honest light,
would others
look beyond the obvious
to find the artistry God sees
as he scours all hidden corners
to find promise in the midst of
every undercover angle
love us unconditionally,
even through times
of our feeling unlovable,
see our beauty rising from ashes?

would the very ones
withholding the approval that draws out
our greatest 'Christian' performances
be willing
to extend
any of the much-needed grace,
and undeserved favor
that rest in our spiritual submission
planted at the foot of the cross?

are we bold enough
to entrust our true, flaw-bearing narrative
to a merciful Savior,
or
are we too distracted
by an imagined response
that clings to the unrestrained display,
of our heart?

For in him all things were created: things in heaven and on earth, visible and invisible, whether thrones or powers or rulers or authorities; all things have been created through him and for him.

Colossians 1:16 (NIV)

creative space

my happy place
is firmly planted
in creative space
where I play to escape,
navigating mind trips,
sprinting free
on a journey marked by
unbridled explorations
of my truest self,
a wide lens view,
exhausting any
and all possibilities

boundaries cease to exist
revealing emotional shelter
shuttered from the stress
of outside influences

imaginary lush landscapes
cradle every impulse
a soft landing
catching
fallen starbursts
of original thought
that glow in the distance
beaming promise.

In the beginning was the Word, and the Word was with God, and the Word was God. He was with God in the beginning. Through him all things were made; without him nothing was made that has been made. In him was life, and that life was the light of all mankind. The light shines in the darkness, and the darkness has not overcome it.

John 1:1-5 (NIV)

spoken word

When the word of God is shot
into the atmosphere,
through the force
of undoctored verses spit with fury,
it's packing heat
burning intensity
populating dense bars of pure sentiment.

it prompts reflective conviction,
baring the weight of all pain,
fighting off fiery darts of disbelief,
overcoming doubts decrying purpose.

it grips, then gathers, lingering fragments of faith,
restoring strength;
boils to a rapid beat,
a once-cold heart,
pumping hope through spiritual veins,
bringing forth evidence of a new life.

it caresses wounds left exposed
fresh, weathered--salving deep scars,
healing vulnerabilities in need of peace

forsaking all idols,
it untangles deceit,
eliminating error,
shining a light
on the cavernous places,
where shame and secrets hide.

unmuddled understanding
once craving clarity, tramples false doctrines,
revealing,
at the depth of the depth,
the purest form of sacrifice—the only begotten,
outstretched for the beloved.

Sing to the LORD a new song; sing to the LORD,
all the earth. Sing to the LORD, praise his name;
proclaim his salvation day after day. Declare his glory
among the nations, his marvelous deeds
among all peoples.

Psalm 96:1-3 (NIV)

reigning glory

Your glory reigns,
unbridled energy filling every inch
of each sun-splashed sky
wrestling the infinite expanse with ease
to magnify
its unique reflection;
warm hues dance,
springing with glee
from your
golden-red palette
as day takes its final bow,
night sprinkles shimmering stars
reclaiming its royal domain.

your glory
rides every rolling wave
and crashing tide,
pure majesty
that catches my breath
with entrancing urgency
quickening my heart's rhythm,
it leads me to
a sacred place
where my spirit relishes,
finding freedom

my humble heart hides,
awaiting answers
to every question
the root of all hope resides
crowning pure and simple beauty
and my joyous soul abides
conformed to your image.

For to us a child is born, to us a son is given, and the government will be on his shoulders. And he will be called Wonderful Counselor, Mighty God, Everlasting Father, Prince of Peace.

Isaiah 9:6 (NIV)

o come

O Come,
adore the living Savior
Mary's blessed child
Immanuel
God with us
birthed by a miracle made manifest
divine intervention
lovingly given in
the immaculate conception
of our Master's plan
to save mankind

let us sing of His glory
rejoice in new mercies
revealed each time
the morning light
strikes a breathless sky

let us humbly bow
extolling His goodness
offering our abundance
unique gifts
punctuated in a rhapsody
of unending praise;

all honor due
our King of Kings
and Lord of Lords

let the world see Him
know of His virtue
every time they see us
receive love
in the strength
of each embrace
extended by His bride

o come
come let us adore Him,
worship,
Jesus Christ, our Lord.

Start children off on the way they should go, and even when they are old they will not turn from it.

Proverbs 22:6 (NIV)

next round

Each sparring match we have
offers insight,
exposing my resistance
to the passage of time,
each day accelerating more rapidly than the last.

I silently watch you slipping away
from my tightly knit embrace,
fingers embattled
by a tireless grip on the protection I gave freely,
protection your innocence once demanded,
protection you no longer demand or need,
and I panic, sending
emotional shockwaves that showcase
an overworked attempt
to mask my fear of your unknown.

collected tears may blur my view,
but I do see you
claiming your identity,
clearly hear you refining your voice,
defining your character,
becoming a man, your own man,
full knowledge of self
sharpening your understanding of life.

And it all leaves me raw,
bare,
shivering in the absence of cover,
no longer shielded
by a reflection of the image
I've worn for so long.

I'm now forced to rediscover myself
while hanging on tight, with full strength,
to nostalgia,
tracing memories
of every trip to the park, quiet story time
and mommy-son adventure,
suddenly struck by
the weight of each moment
that burrows deep within my heart.

The earth is the LORD's, and everything in it, the world, and all who live in it; for he founded it on the seas and established it on the waters.

Psalm 24:1-2 (NIV)

indigo

The ocean is a poem
without words
imparting profound wisdom,
rich insights
distilled in rising silence
hovering over
the rhythmic motion
of rolling sea foam waves,
mindful rest
in a glistening backdrop,
indigo and serene
that shines perfection
reflecting the white light of sun
absorbing the heat of day,
my toes submerge
eager to soak up warmth
feeling the sound of life
a free-form celebration
pulsing
sharing every nuanced message
as I breathe in the quietness
exhaling peace
bathing
in the muted
hush of the moment.

Whoever dwells in the shelter of the Most High will rest in the shadow of the Almighty. I will say of the Lord, "He is my refuge and my fortress, my God, in whom I trust." Surely he will save you from the fowler's snare and from the deadly pestilence. He will cover you with his feathers, and under his wings you will find refuge; his faithfulness will be your shield and rampart.

Psalm 91:1-4 (NIV)

beyond midnight musings

Unending fear and doubt
cause my heart to linger
in fields of insecurity,
wracked with uncertainty
trapped
an endless mind game,
chasing
ill-conceived, unattainable perfection
evading every part of me

softly, He whispers sweet symphonies
His easily perfected joy and peace
soon released in the earliest morning breeze
easing my anger

the great I AM
serenading me
as I am
restored to rest.

Now faith is confidence in what we hope for and assurance about what we do not see.

Hebrews 1:11 (NIV)

cycle of doubt

Lord, I say I believe in you
yet, every time adversity
applies pressure,
I stumble over old patterns,
tripping on *my* broken promises
for an imagined eternity
numb to any nuance of hope
trapped inside a dizzying mental free fall
without a scriptural filter,

tired eyes
locked on stale impressions
replaying memories
that leave me breathless,
gasping for spiritual oxygen;
silent screams for You escape
a soul chokehold
as I teeter on my wit's end.

without notice,
comfort comes,
mapping reminders
of past deliverance
and doubt gives way,

leading me to
renewed faith.

I fall to my knees and pray,
clinging to *your* promises
believing tomorrow will be better,
but always left exhausted,
wondering,
when this cycle of doubt will end.

Therefore, if anyone is in Christ, the new creation has come: The old has gone, the new is here!

2 Corinthians 5:17 (NIV)

creative anthem

In the presence of my people,
inspiration soars
pouring over me,
drenching all that's arid;
soul nourishment,
extinguishing any foolish attempt
to retreat from my calling.

I am rich with brazen ambition,
poised to write, share, and be heard.
my spirit rises high
on the adrenaline of the moment,
basking in the refined brilliance
that surrounds me.

in the midst of my chosen tribe,
iron sharpens iron,
truth honors truth, and
game recognizes game.

when we creative souls gather,
we fearlessly bear the weight of the world,
trying to make sense
of society's nonsense,

choking on the bitterness
forced down our throats like punishment.

we always do the heavy mental lifting,
collectively challenging injustice
and, when we do,
confusion begins to uncoil, taking shape
around every empowered thought
liberated
on the strength of our pens.

Therefore confess your sins to each other and pray for each other so that you may be healed. The prayer of a righteous person is powerful and effective.

James 5:16 (NIV)

pray

When I pray,
God mends my heart
because it's pliable,
salvaging broken pieces
from every fractured area.

I bow to the Most High God,
putting all interests aside,
acknowledging the Creator of the universe
who reigns.

He readies my spirit,
sweeping away the debris of disobedience
that corrodes hidden places,
filling them instead with a light
that dominates the darkness.
He removes the strain
of shame and guilt
that manifests,
as my soul collapses
under the weight of judgement—my own,
that of others.

He leans in when I cry out,
reassuring me He hears
even the slightest silent plea,
suppressing my pain,
suspending any moment of weakness,

He sharpens my senses
so that I might be more attuned
to the needs of others,
more inclined to bear their burdens
more aware of the concerns of my country,
the world,
willing to stand in the gap for the lost, the fallen.

humbled in His Holy presence,
I have visions of new mercies and
extended grace, unwarranted favor I cannot
explain or fully comprehend.
I sit at His feet,
listen intently,
gathering each pearl He drops
in answer to any reference
of earthly sorrow,
seeking His wisdom
in anticipation of future need.

my soul leaps, invigorated, refreshed,
infused with the hope
that pours from His word,
penetrates my perspective.

when I fall to my knees,
enter into my closet
in submission
putting Him first,
declaring this one-on-one moment sacred,
I am realigned with my purpose
reminded of every provision
He's ever made with divine precision,

when I pray,
knowing He is my source,
I draw on resources
unseen in the natural,
unknown to the blind,
lost in the secular.

when I earnestly come to Him,
all defenses down,
my 'Abba Father Daddy God'
gently takes my hand,
orders my steps
and leads me with all the love needed
to continue my journey in victory.

Looking unto Jesus, the author and finisher of our faith, who for the joy that was set before Him endured the cross, despising the shame, and has sat down at the right hand of the throne of God.

Hebrews 12:2 (NKJV)

what's next?

White noise drowns
the sound of white-knuckle pleas
leaving me
balancing on the very edge of my mind
struggling to inhale fresh creativity,
clinging to the hope of something new
in the midst of all day,
every day,
same ole, same ole'isms

monotony stands on notice
as anticipation
stares straight
into complacency's dead eyes,
shooting electric shocks
splitting the very ends,
of every crowning hair,
demanding change
with a fierce resolve
planted.
echoing a deep utterance
a question--only two words
that rise up from deep within
fling off my tongue,

snap the trap of stagnation
and free me
feeding fuel for renewal
ushering a freshness
that blows in with my second wind

What's next?

Does not wisdom call out? Does not understanding raise her voice? At the highest point along the way, where the paths meet, she takes her stand; beside the gate leading into the city, at the entrance, she cries aloud: "To you, O people, I call out; I raise my voice to all mankind. You who are simple, gain prudence; you who are foolish, set your hearts on it.

Proverbs 8:1-5 (NIV)

honest sojourner

Inspired by Sonia Sanchez

She drums the rhythm
of her heartbeat,
stirring soothing vibrations
in synch with soul stillness
leaving her attuned
to echoed cries
in the open air of oppression

word warrior—honest sojourner
taking great strides in timeless truth
armed with wisdom
that ignites courage,
siphons the strength of our ancestors.

adorned with steel filaments of sacrifice,
she scours any evidence
of blistered resistance unyielding to change.

fierce,
fearless as the night, she reigns
crowned with the wonder
of fresh creativity
spitting fire, fanning flames, blazing trails

mother to all,
she bears the burdens of her people,
parting her lips to feed the world freedom.
they sip, as she spills mental milk and honey,
left hungering for the next course
of language lingering
on the tip of her tongue.

For you created my inmost being; you knit me together in my mother's womb. I praise you because I am fearfully and wonderfully made; your works are wonderful, I know that full well. My frame was not hidden from you when I was made in the secret place, when I was woven together in the depths of the earth. Your eyes saw my unformed body; all the days ordained for me were written in your book before one of them came to be.

Psalm 139: 13-16 (NIV)

affirmation

Inspired by Toni Morrison

I stand on truth
to affirm my humanity,
defiant,
confounding those
who might instead choose
to deny it.

I soar,
expanding my reach
to the full breadth
of my dreams,
flying freely
over the short-sighted,
always lost and left blinded by the brilliance
of my shine.

I balance,
on the steely shoulders
of those who fought bone-tired,
strengthened by conviction;
see my reflection
in the boldness of their resolve;
discover my purpose,

raising the mantle
they inspired even higher.

I write--to keep from screaming--
chronicling blatant hypocrisy
that defines, yet haunts this nation,
puncturing the surface
of false narratives
to expose raw
a deeper layer of the America I know.

I break all constraints
and find freedom
in expression;
revel in my uniqueness,
braiding coarse wisdom
into stories for the ages;
thick, unyielding
bounding down my back,
independence,
wild with abandon.

the power of my voice charges forward
penetrating the consciousness
of future generations
with a force
that easily blows through
any remaining barriers to understanding.

Cause me to understand the way of your precepts,
that I may meditate on your wonderful deeds.
My soul is weary with sorrow; strengthen me
according to your word.

Psalm 119: 27-28 (NIV)

butterfly

On muted days
when the light hides,
blending into its shadow,
darkness hovers,
subduing all that's stuck
in the chasm of life's daily grind.

I wrap myself around myself
in a tightly knit embrace;
an airtight emotional barricade,
that seals me on the inside
from all the elements,
lulls me to peace,
beckoning
a loving brush
with divine intervention.

I piece together strands of hope,
that provide cover
as I wrestle with doubt, drawing deep on faith
to believe, have vision, seize the promise
of what I am unable to see--destiny,
purpose, my expected end.

gradually, the warmth of sun radiates
thawing my emotional frost,
allowing for release,
offering a breath of fresh air
that loosens my stubborn grip.

I stretch my wings,
an endless reach revealing all my colors
that speak life,
flirt with possibility,
extending to influence my atmosphere,
as I take flight and prepare to soar.

But you are a chosen people, a royal priesthood,
a holy nation, God's special possession, that you may
declare the praises of him who called you out of
darkness into his wonderful light.

1 Peter 2:9 (NIV)

she stands

Bold to the point of brazenness,
determined
a boundless spirit
breaking away from any binding ties
that restrict her
moving ahead
taking life-affirming strides

a single step
powered by the stretch
of muscle-toned legs
conditioned under the weight
of the load she's carried;
reaching, striving,
strengthened by
repurposed fatigue
reframing every tiring moment
of her journey.

powerful eyes fasten to the future
glistening with tears of wisdom
reflecting the understanding
of memories unpacked
nourishing the core of her resolution,

making room
embracing each new opportunity,
in the expanse of her new scope of freedom.

The LORD is my light and my salvation—
whom shall I fear? The LORD is the stronghold of
my life—of whom shall I be afraid?

Psalm 27:1

The LORD is my shepherd; I shall not want.

He maketh me to lie down in green pastures:
he leadeth me beside the still waters.

He restoreth my soul: he leadeth me in the paths
of righteousness for his name's sake.

Yea, though I walk through the valley of the shadow
of death, I will fear no evil: for thou art with me;
thy rod and thy staff they comfort me.

Thou preparest a table before me in the presence
of mine enemies: thou anointest my head with oil;
my cup runneth over.

Surely goodness and mercy shall follow me all the days
of my life: and I will dwell in the house of the LORD for ever.

Psalm 23 (KJV)